High Availability for the LAMP Stack

Jason Cannon

Contents

Introduction

One of the most common ways to deliver web applications is through the use of the LAMP stack. LAMP is an acronym that stands for Linux, Apache, MySQL, and PHP. In this design Linux is the operating system, Apache is the web server, MySQL acts as the database, and PHP is used as the programming language. This architecture can be used to host open source applications or custom written web apps. Popular websites like Facebook, Wikipedia, and Yahoo use this design to serve millions of users worldwide. Open source applications such as WordPress, Drupal, Joomla!, MediaWiki, and SugarCRM also rely on the LAMP stack.

Whether you are deploying or supporting a custom written application or using an open source solution, you'll want to employ an architecture that maximizes the availability of that application, eliminates single points of failure, allows you to scale without downtime, and is relatively easy to implement and support. It's better to take the time upfront to account for the requirements and long term goals of the service you're implementing than it is to make architectural decisions during an emergency situation like an expected surge of traffic or an outage. During an emergency is not the best time to be designing solutions.

Each project may have varying requirements, but in general there are few important points to at least consider. They are redundancy, scalability, performance, and manageability. Redundancy is how to tolerate failures. Scalability is how to serve an increasing or decreasing user base. Performance is how to ensure each user's experience is at or beyond an acceptable level. Having a redundant, scalable, performant service means nothing if it's unmanageable or unsupportable, therefore manageability is a key consideration. Who is going to implement the design? Who is going to support it? Is it feasible to scale in the manner laid out in the design? Sometimes more complex solutions can be ruled out due to the lack of resources such as available finances and specialized staff. Also, complex solutions that were designed to decrease downtime can actually increase downtime due to the level of troubleshooting required when something unexpected occurs.

This book lays out a couple of designs that address all the previous points. The designs proposed eliminate single points of failure and can be scaled to serve an increasing number of users with acceptable performance. Designs will be presented that work on physical hardware, virtual servers, and in the cloud. They are relatively simple designs that meet all of those requirements, making them easy to implement, manage, and support.

To download the example configuration files, scripts, and diagrams used in this book visit:
 http://www.linuxtrainingacademy.com/ha-lamp

Preparing a Local Test Environment

If you would like to test the designs presented in this book on your own local workstation before trying them elsewhere, I recommend installing VirtualBox and Vagrant. VirtualBox is virtualization software that allows you to create virtual machines where you can run an operating system (guest) inside your current operating system (host). VirtualBox is supported on Windows, Mac, and Linux. To install it, visit the VirtualBox download page located at https://www.virtualbox.org/wiki/Downloads and grab the installer for your current operating system. Click through the install screens and accept the defaults.

Vagrant is software that allows you to easily create virtual test and development environments. You can think of it as a wrapper around virtualization software such as VirtualBox. It also supports other virtualization software and providers such as VMware, Docker, and Amazon Web Services (AWS). To install Vagrant, first download the appropriate installer package for your operating system from https://www.vagrantup.com/downloads.html. Next, launch the installer and accept the defaults. After Vagrant is installed you will be able to access the `vagrant` command from the command line.

If you are going to be using Windows as your host operating system you can optionally install a command line SSH client. Vagrant can easily connect you to the virtual machines it creates if it has access to an SSH utility. Mac and Linux users already have a built in command line client. If you don't install one for Windows you will have to manually connect to the virtual machines it creates. You can use Putty (http://www.linuxtrainingacademy.com/putty/) or any other SSH client that you desire for this purpose. If you do want a command line SSH client for windows you can download and install git (http://www.git-scm.com). Be sure to select "Use Git and optional Unix tools from the Windows Command Prompt" during the install. Your other option is to install Cygwin from https://www.cygwin.com.

A Crash Course in Vagrant

Here is a list of commonly used vagrant commands.

`vagrant init [box-name] [box-url]` - Initializes the current directory to be a Vagrant environment and creates the Vagrant configuration file `Vagrantfile`.

`vagrant up` - This command creates, configures, and starts the virtual machine defined in the `Vagrantfile`. If the virtual machine already exists, it simply starts it.

`vagrant halt` - Stops a virtual machine.

`vagrant destroy` - Deletes the virtual machine.

`vagrant ssh` - Connects to the virtual machine via SSH.

In the following example I am going to create a directory, or folder, for my Vagrant project. Next I am going to initialize that project, configure a virtual machine, launch it, and finally connect to it. The following commands will create a virtual machine that runs Ubuntu 14.04.

Note that the first time you run these series of commands an image of the Ubuntu operating system will be downloaded from the Internet. This can take several minutes to complete. On subsequent runs this process is much quicker as the image used to create the virtual machines will already be stored on your system.

Summary:

```
vagrant init ubuntu/trusty64
vagrant up
vagrant ssh
```

Example:

```
[jason@localbox ~]$ mkdir my-first-test-box
[jason@localbox ~]$ cd my-first-test-box
[jason@localbox ~/my-first-test-box]$ vagrant
init ubuntu/trusty64
A `Vagrantfile` has been placed in this
directory. You are now
ready to `vagrant up` your first virtual
environment! Please read
the comments in the Vagrantfile as well as
documentation on
`vagrantup.com` for more information on using
Vagrant.
[jason@localbox ~/my-first-test-box]$ vagrant up
Bringing machine 'default' up with 'virtualbox'
provider...
```

```
==> default: Importing base box
'ubuntu/trusty64'...
==> default: Matching MAC address for NAT
networking...
==> default: Checking if box 'ubuntu/trusty64' is
up to date...
==> default: Setting the name of the VM: my-
first-test-box_default_1417836197327_31478
==> default: Clearing any previously set
forwarded ports...
==> default: Fixed port collision for 22 => 2222.
Now on port 2204.
==> default: Clearing any previously set network
interfaces...
==> default: Preparing network interfaces based
on configuration...
    default: Adapter 1: nat
==> default: Forwarding ports...
    default: 22 => 2204 (adapter 1)
==> default: Booting VM...
==> default: Waiting for machine to boot. This
may take a few minutes...
    default: SSH address: 127.0.0.1:2204
    default: SSH username: vagrant
    default: SSH auth method: private key
    default: Warning: Connection timeout.
Retrying...
==> default: Machine booted and ready!
==> default: Checking for guest additions in
VM...
==> default: Mounting shared folders...
    default: /vagrant => /home/jason/my-first-
test-box
[jason@localbox ~/my-first-test-box]$ vagrant ssh
Welcome to Ubuntu 14.04.1 LTS (GNU/Linux 3.13.0-
40-generic x86_64)
```

```
  * Documentation:  https://help.ubuntu.com/

   System information as of Sat Dec  6 03:23:33
UTC 2014

   System load:  0.66               Processes:
      90
   Usage of /:   2.7% of 39.34GB    Users logged
in:   0
   Memory usage: 16%                IP address for
eth0: 10.0.2.15
   Swap usage:   0%

   Graph this data and manage this system at:
      https://landscape.canonical.com/

   Get cloud support with Ubuntu Advantage Cloud
Guest:
      http://www.ubuntu.com/business/services/clo
ud

0 packages can be updated.
0 updates are security updates.


vagrant@vagrant-ubuntu-trusty-64:~$ exit
[jason@localbox ~/my-first-test-box]$
```

For more information about Vagrant, visit the Vagrant
documentation website at https://docs.vagrantup.com.

To download a copy of the Vagrantfiles used in this book visit:
http://www.linuxtrainingacademy.com/ha-lamp

7

The Design

Before we start to eliminate single points of failure in a system we need to identify all the components that make up that system. Since our goal is to make the LAMP stack highly available we already know that we need to account for Linux, Apache, MySQL, and PHP. However, there are other less obvious components that need to be accounted for in the architecture. Let's start out by looking at the LAMP stack on a single server.

Typical Web Application Residing on a Single Server

A typical web application request looks like this. A user types a web address or URL into a web browser and hits enter. The domain name of the website is translated into an IP address using DNS resolution. The browser then connects to that IP address and requests a web page. The connection is received by the web server. If the website is a static website, the web server reads the HTML file off of the storage device and sends that data back over the network to the requestor. If the website is a dynamic web site or web application, then the web server will do some sort of processing in order to create or build a web page to send back. This processing could include performing computations, requesting data from a database, and/or reading data from a disk in order to create the content that will be delivered back over the network to the requestor.

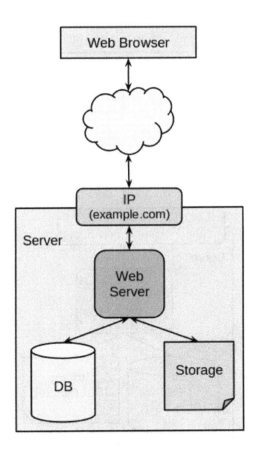

Let's say the service we are deploying is a website powered by WordPress and a user wants to read our latest blog post. The user would request the web page for the blog post which would cause the web server to execute the WordPress PHP code. That would trigger a query to the database to get the content of the blog post as well as any associated comments. The PHP code would then build an HTML document that contained that information and send it to the requestor via the web server. The user's web browser would parse the response and make additional requests to the web server to display the page. For example, if that blog post had a picture of a cat in it, the web browser would request that image causing the web server to read the image data from disk and deliver it back over the network to the web browser.

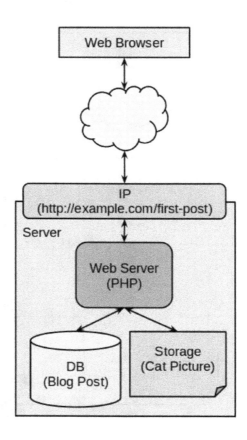

If a single server is performing all of this work, it will have an IP address that corresponds to the website name. It will also be running a web server, a database server, and storing files on some sort of storage device. By examining how a typical request takes place you can see that we will not only need to eliminate the single points of failure for Linux, Apache, MySQL, and PHP, but we will also need to eliminate single points of failure for storage and networking.

But before we get into how to do that, let's look at availability and scalability.

Scaling VS Availability

Vertical Scaling

You can scale without increasing availability or uptime. Let's say you want to handle more users, more traffic, and more load for your web application. If it's a physical server, you could power off the server, install more memory and upgrade the CPUs, for instance. You could also copy all of your data from a single small server to a larger server that has more memory, more CPUs, and faster storage. If you're running a virtual server you could stop the server, allocate more resources to it and start it up again. If your server is running in the cloud you could change your instance type to one that has more resources. This is called vertical scaling, or scaling up. There is nothing wrong with this method of scaling, especially if you have an application where downtime is acceptable.

Horizontal Scaling

Another way to scale is to add more servers, which you'll sometimes hear referred to as nodes. This is called horizontal scaling or scaling out. In order to scale horizontally you'll need to do a bit of upfront work and design for it. In order to go from one web server, for instance, to two web servers you'll need a way to route traffic to the additional node and preferably spread that load between the two servers. If you need more resources, add a third or fourth server. When you only have one server and it goes down you have a service outage, but if you have several servers performing the same function and one of them goes down the worst case scenario is that the service is degraded and doesn't perform as well as it typically does. The best case scenario is having a single failure be practically unnoticeable.

The Best of Both Worlds

In many cases it makes sense to scale your web servers horizontally while you scale your database servers vertically. Next, we'll cover how to get the best of both worlds while eliminating, or at least greatly reducing, the downtime for your service.

The High Availability Architecture

This diagram shows the architecture deployed on a total of five servers. Three servers will act as a database cluster while the other two servers will run the remaining services. Running multiple services on a single node is sometimes referred to as pancaking. We'll first deploy the multiple services on two nodes and afterwards discuss how these services can be broken up, run across various numbers of servers, and scaled.

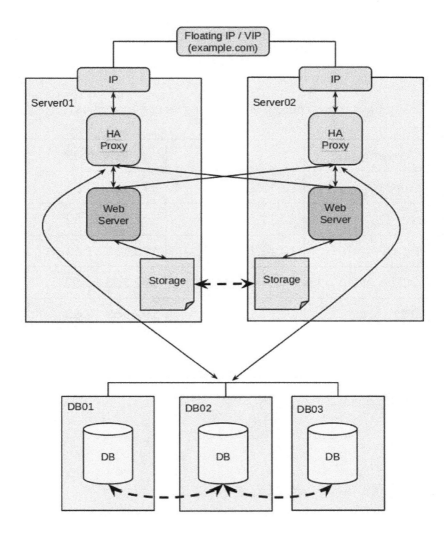

Building the Servers (Vagrant Configuration)

To create a local test environment and deploy the servers for this architecture, use the following Vagrantfile. Remember to create a directory specifically for this Vagrantfile and run the associated vagrant commands from within that directory.

To download these as well as the other configuration files used throughout this book visit:
http://www.linuxtrainingacademy.com/ha-lamp

This configuration creates the following virtual machines:

Server Name	Public IP	Private IP
server01	10.11.12.51	192.168.12.51
server02	10.11.12.52	192.168.12.52
db01	10.11.12.61	192.168.12.61
db02	10.11.12.62	192.168.12.62
db03	10.11.12.63	192.168.12.63

```
VAGRANTFILE_API_VERSION = "2"

Vagrant.configure(VAGRANTFILE_API_VERSION) do
|config|
  config.vm.define "server01" do |server01|
    server01.vm.box = "ubuntu/trusty64"
    server01.vm.hostname = "server01"
    server01.vm.network :private_network, ip:
"10.11.12.51"
    server01.vm.network :private_network, ip:
"192.168.12.51", virtualbox__intnet: true
  end

  config.vm.define "server02" do |server02|
    server02.vm.box = "ubuntu/trusty64"
    server02.vm.hostname = "server02"
```

```
      server02.vm.network :private_network, ip:
"10.11.12.52"
      server02.vm.network :private_network, ip:
"192.168.12.52", virtualbox__intnet: true
  end

  config.vm.define "db01" do |db01|
      db01.vm.box = "ubuntu/trusty64"
      db01.vm.hostname = "db01"
      db01.vm.network :private_network, ip:
"10.11.12.61"
      db01.vm.network :private_network, ip:
"192.168.12.61", virtualbox__intnet: true
  end

  config.vm.define "db02" do |db02|
      db02.vm.box = "ubuntu/trusty64"
      db02.vm.hostname = "db02"
      db02.vm.network :private_network, ip:
"10.11.12.62"
      db02.vm.network :private_network, ip:
"192.168.12.62", virtualbox__intnet: true
  end

  config.vm.define "db03" do |db03|
      db03.vm.box = "ubuntu/trusty64"
      db03.vm.hostname = "db03"
      db03.vm.network :private_network, ip:
"10.11.12.63"
      db03.vm.network :private_network, ip:
"192.168.12.63", virtualbox__intnet: true
  end

  config.vm.provider :virtualbox do |vb|
      vb.customize ["modifyvm", :id, "--memory",
"320"]
  end
```

```
end
```

Run the following commands to create the virtual machines.

```
$ mkdir halamp
$ cd halamp
$ vi Vagrantfile    # Use your favorite editor
$ vagrant up
```

To connect to a specific virtual machine supply it's name after the vagrant ssh command. Here are a couple of examples:

```
$ vagrant ssh server01
$ vagrant ssh db02
```

Configuring High Availability for the IP Address

To eliminate the single point of failure for the DNS name of the website we will create a floating IP, or virtual IP (VIP), that can be assigned to either of the front end servers. It will only be associated with one server at a time. If the server it is associated with fails, the IP will "float" over to the other server. We will use Keepalived to implement the floating IP. Keepalived uses VRRP (Virtual Router Redundancy Protocol) to control the VIP. This design works well when you are using physical or virtual servers. We'll cover how to handle this single point of failure in the cloud in the a bit later.

You will need to perform these actions on both of the front end servers in order to install Keepalived.

```
vagrant@server01:~$ sudo apt-get install -y
keepalived
```

```
vagrant@server02:~$ sudo apt-get install -y
keepalived
```

On server01, use the following configuration in the
/etc/keepalived/keepalived.conf file.

```
vrrp_script chk_haproxy {
      script "killall -0 haproxy"
      interval 2                              # check
every 2 seconds
}

vrrp_instance VI_1 {
      state MASTER
      interface eth1
      virtual_router_id 51
      priority 101
      vrrp_unicast_bind 192.168.12.51   #
Internal IP of this machine
      vrrp_unicast_peer 192.168.12.52   #
Internal IP of peer
      virtual_ipaddress {
            10.11.12.50 dev eth1 label eth1:vip1
      }
      track_script {
            chk_haproxy weight 2
      }
}
```

On server02, use the following configuration in the
/etc/keepalived/keepalived.conf file.

```
vrrp_script chk_haproxy {
      script "killall -0 haproxy"
      interval 2                              # check
every 2 seconds
}
```

```
vrrp_instance VI_1 {
     state BACKUP
     interface eth1
     virtual_router_id 51
     priority 100
     vrrp_unicast_bind 192.168.12.52    #
Internal IP of this machine
     vrrp_unicast_peer 192.168.12.51    #
Internal IP of peer
     virtual_ipaddress {
          10.11.12.50 dev eth1 label eth1:vip1
     }
     track_script {
          chk_haproxy weight 2
     }
}
```

This configuration uses unicast for VRRP instead of the default multicast. This configuration will work where multicast is not enabled, reliable, or supported. This type of situation is common in virtual environments. Assign the private IP of the server to **vrrp_unicast_bind** and the private IP of the other server to **vrrp_unicast_peer**. The virtual IP in this example is 10.11.12.50.

Also be aware that the router ID needs to be the same on all the nodes. The priority of the master server should be higher than the backup server. The server with the highest priority will be assigned the VIP. In this configuration we used a priority of 101 for the master and 100 for the backup node. If HAProxy is functioning properly the priority is adjusted by its weight. If both nodes are functioning normally server01 will have a priority of 103 (101 + 2), while server02 will have a priority of 102 (100 + 2). If HAProxy were to die on server01 it's priority would go down to 100, making server02's priority higher. In this situation the VIP would be removed from server01 and associated to server02.

Let's start the service on each of the nodes and check to see if the VIP is assigned to server01 like we expect.

```
vagrant@server01:~$ sudo service keepalived start
vagrant@server02:~$ sudo service keepalived start
```

At this point you should be able to ping the VIP, or floating IP, and it should be assigned to the primary server.

```
vagrant@server01:~$ ip addr show eth1
3: eth1: <BROADCAST,MULTICAST,UP,LOWER_UP> mtu
1500 qdisc pfifo_fast state UP group default qlen
1000
       link/ether 08:00:27:b8:c7:c9 brd
ff:ff:ff:ff:ff:ff
       inet 10.11.12.51/24 brd 10.11.12.255 scope
global eth1
       valid_lft forever preferred_lft forever
       inet 10.11.12.50/32 scope global eth1:vip1
       valid_lft forever preferred_lft forever
       inet6 fe80::a00:27ff:feb8:c7c9/64 scope
link
       valid_lft forever preferred_lft forever
```

You can verify connectivity to the VIP by pinging it from your workstation.

```
[jason@localbox]$ ping -c 3 10.11.12.50
PING 10.11.12.50 (10.11.12.50) 56(84) bytes of
data.
64 bytes from 10.11.12.50: icmp_seq=1 ttl=64
time=0.305 ms
```

```
64 bytes from 10.11.12.50: icmp_seq=2 ttl=64
time=0.380 ms
64 bytes from 10.11.12.50: icmp_seq=3 ttl=64
time=0.427 ms

--- 10.11.12.50 ping statistics ---
3 packets transmitted, 3 received, 0% packet
loss, time 2000ms
rtt min/avg/max/mdev = 0.305/0.370/0.427/0.054 ms
```

Note, the **ping** command will look like the following on a Windows machine. **ping 10.11.12.50**

To ensure that the failover is working properly we can simulate a failure on the primary server by downing (stopping) the network interface the VIP is associated with. You can start a ping to the VIP in another terminal or window while you simulate the failure if you'd like.

```
[jason@localbox]$ ping 10.11.12.50
PING 10.11.12.50 (10.11.12.50) 56(84) bytes of
data.
64 bytes from 10.11.12.50: icmp_seq=1 ttl=64
time=0.305 ms
...

$ vagrant ssh server01
vagrant@server01:~$ ip link set eth1 down
```

On server01 you will see something like this in **/var/log/syslog**.

```
Dec  4 04:57:58 server01 Keepalived_vrrp[2227]:
Kernel is reporting: interface eth1 DOWN
Dec  4 04:57:58 server01 Keepalived_vrrp[2227]:
VRRP_Instance(VI_1) Entering FAULT STATE
```

```
Dec  4 04:57:58 server01 Keepalived_vrrp[2227]:
VRRP_Instance(VI_1) Now in FAULT state
```

On server02 you will see something like this in
/var/log/syslog:

```
Dec  4 05:00:02 vagrant-ubuntu-trusty-64
Keepalived_vrrp[4071]: VRRP_Instance(VI_1)
Transition to MASTER STATE
Dec  4 05:00:03 vagrant-ubuntu-trusty-64
Keepalived_vrrp[4071]: VRRP_Instance(VI_1)
Entering MASTER STATE
```

If you have a ping command running in the background it still should
be responding to pings. You could also start a new ping to ensure
the VIP is reachable.

```
[jason@localbox]$ ping -c 3 10.11.12.50
PING 10.11.12.50 (10.11.12.50) 56(84) bytes of
data.
64 bytes from 10.11.12.50: icmp_seq=1 ttl=64
time=0.305 ms
64 bytes from 10.11.12.50: icmp_seq=2 ttl=64
time=0.380 ms
64 bytes from 10.11.12.50: icmp_seq=3 ttl=64
time=0.427 ms

--- 10.11.12.50 ping statistics ---
3 packets transmitted, 3 received, 0% packet
loss, time 2000ms
rtt min/avg/max/mdev = 0.305/0.370/0.427/0.054 ms
```

When you bring the network interface back up on the primary
server back it will take back the VIP. If you want to prevent this
behavior use the **nopreempt** option in **keepalived.conf**.

```
vagrant@server01:~$ ip link set eth1 up
```

On server01 you will see something like this in
/var/log/syslog:

```
Dec  4 05:01:08 server01 Keepalived_vrrp[2227]:
VRRP_Instance(VI_1) prio is higher than received
advert
Dec  4 05:01:08 server01 Keepalived_vrrp[2227]:
VRRP_Instance(VI_1) Transition to MASTER STATE
Dec  4 05:01:09 server01 Keepalived_vrrp[2227]:
VRRP_Instance(VI_1) Entering MASTER STATE
```

On server02 you will see something like this in
/var/log/syslog:

```
Dec  4 05:03:15 vagrant-ubuntu-trusty-64
Keepalived_vrrp[4071]: VRRP_Instance(VI_1)
Received higher prio advert
Dec  4 05:03:15 vagrant-ubuntu-trusty-64
Keepalived_vrrp[4071]: VRRP_Instance(VI_1)
Entering BACKUP STATE
```

Installing and Configuring a Load Balancer

HAProxy will act as the load balancer. We will install it on the front
end nodes using the following commands.

```
vagrant@server01:~$ sudo apt-get install -y
haproxy
vagrant@server02:~$ sudo apt-get install -y
haproxy
```

Use the following configuration in **/etc/haproxy/haproxy.cfg** on both of the front end nodes.

```
global
      log 127.0.0.1 local0 notice
      user haproxy
      group haproxy


defaults
      log   global
      option   dontlognull
      retries 3
      option redispatch
      timeout connect  5000
      timeout client  50000
      timeout server  50000

frontend http
      bind *:80
      mode http
      option httplog
      default_backend webservers

backend webservers
      mode http
      stats enable
      stats uri /haproxy/stats
      stats auth admin:admin
      stats hide-version
      balance roundrobin
      option httpclose
      option forwardfor
      cookie SRVNAME insert
      server server01 192.168.12.51:8080 check
cookie server01
```

```
        server server02 192.168.12.52:8080 check
cookie server02

frontend sql
        bind *:3306
        mode tcp
        option tcplog
        default_backend dbservers

backend dbservers
        balance leastconn
        option httpchk
        server db01 192.168.12.61:3306 check port
9200 inter 12000 rise 3 fall 3
        server db02 192.168.12.62:3306 check port
9200 inter 12000 rise 3 fall 3 backup
        server db03 192.168.12.63:3306 check port
9200 inter 12000 rise 3 fall 3 backup
```

This configuration accepts traffic on the default HTTP port of 80 and proxies it to one of the web servers over the private network. In some cases this will be the same node as the VIP is associated with and the HAProxy process handling the request. In other instances, it will not. It's important to note that one HAProxy instance can handle many backend servers. If we want to add more web servers we can bring them online, add their information into the **haproxy.cfg** file, and reload HAProxy.

For the web traffic we are using the round robin balancing algorithm with sticky sessions. If we were just using round robin the first web request would be routed to the first web server (server01), the second request routed to the second web server (server02), the third request routed to the first web server (server01), etc. This can cause problems for web applications that do not share session information, for example.

Instead of strictly using round robin for each request we use round robin for each session. For example, if Jane visits our website she will get routed to server01. HAProxy will set a cookie containing the web server it routed the initial request to. This cookie will be sent back in subsequent requests from Jane, letting HAProxy know which server to send her requests to. Next, John visits our website and is routed to server02 since it's next in the round robin. The cookie is set and John continues to get routed to server02. The next user will be routed to server01, and so on. Of course, if server01 were to die Jane's requests would be routed to another available server, in this case server02, and the cookie would be reassigned.

In addition to web traffic we'll be using HAProxy to route requests to the database servers. To do this we will have HAProxy listening on the default MySQL port of 3306. It will route requests based on the leastconn algorithm. This means that whichever database server has the least number of connections at the time a request is made is the database server that request is routed to. If all of the database servers have the same number of connections then round robin is used to select the database server. The leastconn algorithm is recommended for "long" sessions that you will encounter when using SQL, LDAP, etc. We'll get into how the health checks work when we configure the database servers.

To enable HAProxy set ENABLED=1 in **/etc/default/haproxy**. Feel free to use your favorite editor to make that change or use the following one-liner which creates a backup of the file named **haproxy.orig** and makes the change.

```
vagrant@server01:~$ sudo sed -i.orig
's/ENABLED=.*/ENABLED=1/' /etc/default/haproxy
vagrant@server01:~$ sudo sed -i.orig
's/ENABLED=.*/ENABLED=1/' /etc/default/haproxy
```

We have configured HAProxy to log to the localhost. Now we need to configure rsyslog to accept those log messages by listening on UDP:514. Create **/etc/rsyslog.d/udp-localhost.conf** and add the following lines to that file.

```
$ModLoad imudp
$UDPServerRun 514
$UDPServerAddress 127.0.0.1
```

Let's reload rsyslog so that it picks up this new configuration.

```
vagrant@server01:~$ sudo service rsyslog restart
vagrant@server02:~$ sudo service rsyslog restart
```

We're ready to start HAproxy.

```
vagrant@server01:~$ sudo service haproxy start
vagrant@server02:~$ sudo service haproxy start
```

You can now view the HAProxy stats of server01 by visiting http://10.11.12.51/haproxy/stats and the stats of server02 by visiting http://10.11.12.52/haproxy/stats. I used a rather insecure username and password of admin:admin, so feel free to update the haproxy.cfg and change those values. Also, you can access the status page using the VIP and whichever server is associated with the VIP will respond. At this point the web servers and database servers will be correctly reported as DOWN since we haven't configured them yet.

Installing and Configuring Apache and PHP

Now that HAProxy is poised to accept web requests, let's install the Apache web server and PHP programming language. Since we'll be connecting to MySQL, we'll need the MySQL module for PHP.

```
vagrant@server01:~$ sudo apt-get install -y
apache2 php5 php5-mysql
vagrant@server02:~$ sudo apt-get install -y
apache2 php5 php5-mysql
```

When you perform the installation you'll likely seen an error like the following one when Apache is started.

```
(98)Address already in use: AH00073: make_sock:
unable to listen for connections on address
0.0.0.0:80
```

This error occurs because HAProxy is already using port 80. If we want to run Apache and HAProxy on the same host we'll need to configure Apache to use a different port. To do that, edit **/etc/apache2/ports.conf** and change Listen 80 to Listen 8080. Here are the contents of **/etc/apache2/ports.conf** after this change.

```
# If you just change the port or add more ports
here, you will likely also
# have to change the VirtualHost statement in
# /etc/apache2/sites-enabled/000-default.conf

#Listen 80
Listen 8080

<IfModule ssl_module>
     Listen 443
</IfModule>

<IfModule mod_gnutls.c>
```

```
    Listen 443
</IfModule>
```

Let's start apache on this new port.

```
vagrant@server01:~$ sudo service apache2 start
vagrant@server02:~$ sudo service apache2 start
```

We can now see that HAProxy is listening on ports 80 and 3306 while apache is listening on port 8080.

```
vagrant@server01:~$ sudo netstat -ntlp | egrep
'haproxy|apache'
tcp    0   0 0.0.0.0:3306    0.0.0.0:*    LISTEN
       1178/haproxy
tcp    0   0 0.0.0.0:80      0.0.0.0:*    LISTEN
       1178/haproxy
tcp6   0   0 :::8080         :::*         LISTEN
       2679/apache2
```

At this point the HAProxy stats page will show that it can communicate to the web servers and that they are up. We can demonstrate that HAProxy is performing the round robin by making HTTP requests. The first request (session) will go to server01 and HAProxy will set the SRVNAME cookie to server01. The second request (session) will go to server02 and HAProxy will set the SRVNAME cookie to server02. Using the -I option to curl just displays the HTTP header information. We're not interested in the actual HTML content for this test.

In this example curl doesn't act like your normal graphical web browser in the sense that when a cookie is set curl doesn't save it and reuse it for subsequent requests. This is why repeated curl requests will demonstrate the round robin in action.

```
[jason@localbox ~]$ curl -I http://10.11.12.50
HTTP/1.1 200 OK
Date: Sat, 06 Dec 2014 16:22:15 GMT
Server: Apache/2.4.7 (Ubuntu)
Connection: close
Content-Type: text/html; charset=UTF-8
Set-Cookie: SRVNAME=server01; path=/

[jason@localbox ~]$ curl -I http://10.11.12.50
HTTP/1.1 200 OK
Date: Sat, 06 Dec 2014 16:22:17 GMT
Server: Apache/2.4.7 (Ubuntu)
Connection: close
Content-Type: text/html;charset=UTF-8
Set-Cookie: SRVNAME=server02; path=/
```

Now let's make curl behave like a typical user's web browser and send back the cookie. We'll make an initial request to get the value of the cookie and then make all the subsequent requests with that cookie value. To make curl send a cookie use **-b "cookie-name:cookie-value"**. If you look at the HAProxy stats page using the VIP you'll see the total sessions number increment each time a request is made.

```
[jason@localbox ~]$ curl -I http://10.11.12.50
HTTP/1.1 200 OK
Date: Sat, 06 Dec 2014 16:23:15 GMT
Server: Apache/2.4.7 (Ubuntu)
Connection: close
Content-Type: text/html; charset=UTF-8
Set-Cookie: SRVNAME=server01; path=/

[jason@localbox ~]$ curl -b "SRVNAME=server01" -I
http://10.11.12.50
HTTP/1.1 200 OK
```

```
Date: Sat, 06 Dec 2014 16:23:17 GMT
Server: Apache/2.4.7 (Ubuntu)
Connection: close
Content-Type: text/html; charset=UTF-8

[jason@localbox ~]$ curl -b "SRVNAME=server01" -I
http://10.11.12.50
HTTP/1.1 200 OK
Date: Sat, 06 Dec 2014 16:23:19 GMT
Server: Apache/2.4.7 (Ubuntu)
Connection: close
Content-Type: text/html; charset=UTF-8
```

HAProxy is routing requests properly and Apache is responding.
Now let's create an Apache configuration file for our web
application. In this example we will use WordPress. Create
/etc/apache2/sites-available/wordpress.conf with
the following contents.

```
LogFormat "%{X-Forwarded-For}i %l %u %t \"%r\"
%>s %b \"%{Referer}i\" \"%{User-Agent}i\""
haproxy_combined

<virtualhost *:8080>
  DocumentRoot /var/www/wordpress

  <Location />
     Options -Indexes
  </Location>

  ErrorLog ${APACHE_LOG_DIR}/wordpress_error.log
  LogLevel warn
  CustomLog
${APACHE_LOG_DIR}/wordpress_access.log
haproxy_combined
</virtualhost>
```

The configuration takes into account that HAProxy will always be making requests to Apache. In this architecture the end users do not and should not make requests directly to a particular web server. If we used the default logging configuration the web server logs would only contain the IP addresses of the HAProxy servers and we would have no idea where the connections actually originated from. HAProxy, and most other proxies, set an X-Forwarded-For header that contains the IP address of the original requestor. We update the Apache log format to use that instead IP instead of the IP of the proxies.

Let's enable this configuration and disable the default configuration. Also let's enable mod_rewrite for Wordpress.

```
vagrant@server01:~$ sudo a2ensite wordpress
vagrant@server01:~$ sudo a2dissite 000-default
vagrant@server01:~$ sudo a2enmod rewrite


vagrant@server02:~$ sudo a2ensite wordpress
vagrant@server02:~$ sudo a2dissite 000-default
vagrant@server02:~$ sudo a2enmod rewrite
```

Now we can have Apache reload the configuration.

```
vagrant@server01:~$ sudo service apache2 reload
vagrant@server02:~$ sudo service apache2 reload
```


Installing and Configuring Highly Available Storage

If your web application only contains static files and no data is written to disk you can populate the file system on each web server with the exact same contents. However, in the case of WordPress it uses the file system to store uploaded media, plugins, and themes. You don't want to create a blog post featuring your favorite picture of your cat only to get stored on the web server you were connected to at the time you created the post. If this were to happen some of the website visitors would get to see your lovely cat while others would not. An ever worse scenario would be that you installed a plugin and your website would only function for the users that got routed to the web server with that plugin on the file system.

To get around these problems we need to ensure the contents of the file system for the web application and its data are synced across all the web server nodes. We also need to implement a solution that eliminates single points of failure. GlusterFS is a distributed file system that is scalable, redundant, and easy to manage. Also, it's fairly easy to add additional storage on the fly so you don't have to worry about running out of space or taking downtime.

First, let's prepare some storage to be used by Gluster. In this example we are going to be using disks presented to our servers specifically for Gluster data storage. By default Gluster will not allow you to store data on the same disk as the operating system, but this can be overridden if you want.

To attach a new disk to your VirtualBox virtual machine, first power off the machine. Go to the settings for the virtual machine and navigate to the storage section. Click the "Add Hard Disk" button. Choose, "Create a new disk." Fill out the fields to create the disk. When you power on the virtual machine the newly created disk will be available to Linux.

Gluster recommends using XFS for the file system of the disks it will use. So, let's install support for that.

```
vagrant@server01:~$ sudo apt-get install -y
xfsprogs
vagrant@server02:~$ sudo apt-get install -y
xfsprogs
```

Next we'll need to create an XFS file system on the disk we will be using for Gluster data. Since Gluster relies heavily on extended attributes we need to increase the inode size to 512. In this example the operating system is installed on /dev/sda and /dev/sdb is available to be used.

```
vagrant@server01:~$ sudo mkfs.xfs -i size=512 -f
/dev/sdb
vagrant@server02:~$ sudo mkfs.xfs -i size=512 -f
/dev/sdb
```

Let's create a mount point for our Gluster disk, add an entry for it in /etc/fstab, and mount it.

```
vagrant@server01:~$ echo "/dev/sdb
/data/glusterfs/var-www/brick01 xfs defaults 0 0"
| sudo tee -a /etc/fstab
vagrant@server01:~$ sudo mkdir -p
/data/glusterfs/var-www/brick01
vagrant@server01:~$ sudo mount
/data/glusterfs/var-www/brick01

vagrant@server02:~$ echo "/dev/sdb
/data/glusterfs/var-www/brick02 xfs defaults 0 0"
| sudo tee -a /etc/fstab
vagrant@server02:~$ sudo mkdir -p
/data/glusterfs/var-www/brick02
vagrant@server02:~$ sudo mount
/data/glusterfs/var-www/brick02
```

You'll notice that I used "var-www" in the path. That will be the name of our Gluster volume. We will mount the gluster volume on each of our web servers. You'll also notice that I used the word "brick" in the path. Gluster calls the file systems it uses for storage bricks. Volumes are made up of one or more bricks. If you want to increase the amount of available space in a volume simply add more bricks.

Before we create our Gluster cluster, let's configure the **/etc/hosts** file of each of our nodes so we can communicate with them by name. This is optional, but for me it can be easier to remember server01-private than it is to remember 192.168.12.51. Append the following to the **/etc/hosts** file.

```
# Floating IP
10.11.12.50 vip

# Public Addresses
10.11.12.51 server01
10.11.12.52 server02
10.11.12.61 db01
10.11.12.62 db02
10.11.12.63 db03

# Private Addresses
192.168.12.51 server01-private
192.168.12.52 server02-private
192.168.12.61 db01-private
192.168.12.62 db02-private
192.168.12.63 db03-private
```

Let's install the Gluster server software on both of our front end nodes.

```
vagrant@server01:~$ sudo apt-get install -y
glusterfs-server
```

```
vagrant@server01:~$ sudo apt-get install -y
glusterfs-server
```

To create a Gluster cluster simply peer with the other server or
servers you want to be in your cluster. You'll only need to run the
gluster peer probe command from one of your servers. To
check the status of your cluster use the **gluster peer status**
command. When you run that command it will tell you about the
other peer(s) in the cluster.

```
vagrant@server01:~$ sudo gluster peer probe
server02-private
vagrant@server01:~$ sudo gluster peer status
Number of Peers: 1

Hostname: server02-private
Uuid: 17d644e3-2b2c-4509-987d-9793b46a4a60
State: Peer in Cluster (Connected)

vagrant@server02:~$ sudo gluster peer status
Number of Peers: 1

Hostname: server01-private
Port: 24007
Uuid: 032d946d-e131-455e-a53a-bbc30bc4a3e3
State: Peer in Cluster (Connected)
```

Now that we have a cluster and some bricks, we can create a
volume. We want to be able to survive a single failure, so we'll need
two copies of our data. We do that by creating a replicated volume
and telling Gluster what bricks we want to use for that volume.
We'll use one brick on server01 and another brick on server02. You
can use two different bricks attached to the same server, but this
would not protect us from an entire server going down. If you
attempt to do that Gluster reminds of you this fact and gives you
the option to proceed or cancel.

When you create a volume on one of the nodes in the Gluster cluster the other nodes will become aware of it as well, so you only need to run this command once.

```
vagrant@server01:~$ sudo gluster volume create
var-www replica 2 transport tcp server01-
private:/data/glusterfs/var-www/brick01/brick
server02-private:/data/glusterfs/var-
www/brick02/brick
```

You might have noticed that I used a subdirectory of **brick** within each file system. This will cause the brick to fail if the file system is not mounted. We would rather correctly mark the brick as unavailable instead of possibly writing data to the root volume of the operating system.

After the volume is created you can start it with the following command.

```
vagrant@server01:~$ sudo gluster volume start
var-www
```

You can check the configuration by running this command.

```
vagrant@server01:~$ sudo gluster volume info
```

```
Volume Name: var-www
Type: Replicate
Volume ID: d4817936-695c-49ca-88a5-78527ddec8fc
Status: Started
Number of Bricks: 1 x 2 = 2
Transport-type: tcp
Bricks:
Brick1: server01-private:/data/glusterfs/var-
www/brick01/brick
```

```
Brick2: server02-private:/data/glusterfs/var-
www/brick02/brick
```

We want to mount the volume at boot time, so we'll need to add an entry into the **/etc/fstab** file on each of the front end nodes. For server01, use this entry:

```
server01-private:/var-www /var/www glusterfs
defaults,_netdev,fetch-attempts=5 0 0
```

On server02, use this entry:

```
server02-private:/var-www /var/www glusterfs
defaults,_netdev,fetch-attempts=5 0 0
```

Note that even though we specified the host itself in the **/etc/fstab** file Gluster knows about all the members of the cluster that have the data for that volume. Gluster stores this data on the client in something called a volume file. In this configuration our Gluster servers are also Gluster clients, but this doesn't have to be the case and it still works in the same manner. If the disk used to host the brick on server01 fails, server01 will seamless get its data for **/var/www** from server02 since it knows it is part of the cluster and has the data. The **fetch-attempts=5** option tells Gluster to repeatedly attempt to fetch the volume file(s). It is typically used when there are multiple IP addresses on a server as in our example. Also, **_netdev** signals that networking needs to be started before the file system mount is even attempted.

Before we start using our Gluster volume, let's stop Apache and move the original **/var/www** directory out of the way. If we don't, we will mount over the existing data. You could also remove the contents of this directory or even copy the contents to the volume if you wanted to preserve the data. We'll run these commands on both of the nodes.

```
vagrant@server01:~$ sudo service apache2 stop
vagrant@server01:~$ sudo mv /var/www{,.orig}
vagrant@server01:~$ sudo mkdir /var/www
vagrant@server01:~$ sudo mount /var/www
vagrant@server01:~$ sudo service apache2 start

vagrant@server02:~$ sudo service apache2 stop
vagrant@server02:~$ sudo mv /var/www{,.orig}
vagrant@server02:~$ sudo mkdir /var/www
vagrant@server02:~$ sudo mount /var/www
vagrant@server02:~$ sudo service apache2 start
```

Now the contents **/var/www** will be the same on each of the
servers. We can quickly test this by creating a file from each of the
servers and checking for their existence.

```
vagrant@server01:~$ sudo touch /var/www/from-server01

vagrant@server02:~$ sudo touch /var/www/from-server02

vagrant@server01:~$ ls -l /var/www
total 0
-rw-r--r-- 1 root root 0 Dec  6 22:56 from-
server01
-rw-r--r-- 1 root root 0 Dec  6 22:56 from-
server02
```

Installing and Configuring the Database

We are going to use Percona XtraDB Cluster to provide the high
availability for the database layer. It's based on Percona Server
which is a drop-in replacement for MySQL that provides better
performance than MySQL. Percona XtraDB Cluster also

incorporates Percona XtraBackup which allows for non-blocking backups of your databases. Finally, Galera is used to provide the multimaster (active/active) clustering capabilities.

In most MySQL high availability designs there will be a master server and one or more slaves. Scalability is achieved by adding more slaves, but those slaves are read only copies. Only the master server can accept and process write requests. This means that your web application needs to send database reads to one location and database writes to another. If you're using a custom written application you'll have to do this yourself. Some existing web applications already provide this functionality so it's not an issue. For example, to do this with WordPress you would install and configure the HyperDB plugin. In any case, using Percona XtraDB Cluster avoids this complication altogether.

We are going to use three nodes for the database cluster so it can determine a quorum. If a node in the cluster cannot be reached it means that the node failed or it's still functioning but there is a network connectivity issue. If you were to have a two node cluster and had a network connectivity failure between those nodes, but network connectivity to the clients was still in place and they both committed updates you would end up with diverged data sets. One node would have some data and the other node would have other data. This is called split brain.

Percona XtraDB Cluster guards you against split brain and network partitioning events. If it cannot determine a majority then no nodes in the cluster will process requests. That's better than split brain, but it's effectively a single point of failure. Remember this when you want to horizontally scale your database cluster. Always use an odd number of nodes. There is another option, however. You can use garbd, the Galera Arbitrator, to act as a lightweight member of the cluster. It does not process database requests, but it can act as a tie breaker during a network partitioning event. If you use garbd do not run it on one of the database nodes, place it on another server. A good place to run it is on one of the servers that is acting as a load balancer.

To install Percona XtraDB Cluster run the following commands on each of the database nodes. You will be asked to specify a password for the MySQL root user during installation. After we install the software, let's ensure it's before we update the default configuration and setup the cluster.

```
vagrant@db01:~$ sudo apt-get install -y percona-
xtradb-cluster-server percona-xtradb-cluster-
galera-2.x
vagrant@db01:~$ sudo service mysql stop

vagrant@db02:~$ sudo apt-get install -y percona-
xtradb-cluster-server percona-xtradb-cluster-
galera-2.x
vagrant@db02:~$ sudo service mysql stop

vagrant@db03:~$ sudo apt-get install -y percona-
xtradb-cluster-server percona-xtradb-cluster-
galera-2.x
vagrant@db03:~$ sudo service mysql stop
```

The contents of **/etc/mysql/my.cnf** will be almost identical on all of the nodes. The only difference will be the value of **wsrep_node_address**. It should be set to the private IP of the node. Remember, you can download these configuration files from http://www.linuxtrainingacademy.com/ha-lamp. Here is the **my.cnf** for db01.

```
[mysqld]
datadir=/var/lib/mysql
```

```
user=mysql

# Path to the Galera library.
wsrep_provider=/usr/lib/libgalera_smm.so

# Cluster connection URL contains the private IPs
all nodes.
wsrep_cluster_address=gcomm://192.168.12.61,192.1
68.12.62,192.168.12.63

# In order for Galera to work correctly binlog
format should be ROW.
binlog_format=ROW

# MyISAM storage engine has only experimental
support
default_storage_engine=InnoDB

# This changes how InnoDB autoincrement locks are
managed and is a requirement for Galera
innodb_autoinc_lock_mode=2

# SST method
wsrep_sst_method=xtrabackup

# Cluster name
wsrep_cluster_name=my_lamp_cluster

# Authentication for SST method
wsrep_sst_auth="sstuser:sstuser"

# db01 private IP address
wsrep_node_address=192.168.12.61
```

Here is the **my.cnf** file for db02.

```
[mysqld]
datadir=/var/lib/mysql
user=mysql

# Path to the Galera library.
wsrep_provider=/usr/lib/libgalera_smm.so

# Cluster connection URL contains the private IPs
of all nodes.
wsrep_cluster_address=gcomm://192.168.12.61,192.1
68.12.62,192.168.12.63

# In order for Galera to work correctly the
binlog format should be ROW.
binlog_format=ROW

# MyISAM storage engine has only experimental
support
default_storage_engine=InnoDB

# This changes how InnoDB autoincrement locks are
managed and is a requirement for Galera
innodb_autoinc_lock_mode=2

# SST method
wsrep_sst_method=xtrabackup

# Cluster name
wsrep_cluster_name=my_lamp_cluster

# Authentication for SST method
wsrep_sst_auth="sstuser:sstuser"

# db02 private IP address
wsrep_node_address=192.168.12.62
```

Here is the **my.cnf** file for db03.

```
[mysqld]
datadir=/var/lib/mysql
user=mysql

# Path to the Galera library.
wsrep_provider=/usr/lib/libgalera_smm.so

# Cluster connection URL contains the private IPs
of all nodes.
wsrep_cluster_address=gcomm://192.168.12.61,192.1
68.12.62,192.168.12.63

# In order for Galera to work correctly the
binlog format should be ROW.
binlog_format=ROW

# MyISAM storage engine has only experimental
support
default_storage_engine=InnoDB

# This changes how InnoDB autoincrement locks are
managed and is a requirement for Galera
innodb_autoinc_lock_mode=2

# SST method
wsrep_sst_method=xtrabackup

# Cluster name
wsrep_cluster_name=my_lamp_cluster
```

```
# Authentication for SST method
wsrep_sst_auth="sstuser:sstuser"

# db03 private IP address
wsrep_node_address=192.168.12.63
```

Bootstrapping the Cluster

Next, we need to bootstrap the cluster. We'll do this on db01.

```
vagrant@db01:~$ sudo service mysql bootstrap-pxc
```

We need to create a user that will perform the state snapshot transfers (SST). A SST occurs when a node joins, or rejoins, the cluster. This process copies the data from one active node in the cluster, called a donor, to the joining node, called a joiner. Here are the commands to create that database user.

```
vagrant@db01:~$ sudo mysql -e "CREATE USER
'sstuser'@'localhost' IDENTIFIED BY 'sstuser';"
vagrant@db01:~$ sudo mysql -e "GRANT RELOAD, LOCK
TABLES, REPLICATION CLIENT ON *.* TO
'sstuser'@'localhost';"
vagrant@db01:~$ sudo mysql -e 'FLUSH PRIVILEGES;'
```

At this point the cluster is up with a single node. You can check the node count using the following command.

```
vagrant@db01:~$ sudo mysql -e "show status like
'wsrep_cluster_size';"
+--------------------+-------+
| Variable_name      | Value |
+--------------------+-------+
| wsrep_cluster_size | 1     |
+--------------------+-------+
```

Next we can bring the other two nodes into the cluster. Let's start MySQL (Percona XtraDB Cluster) on the remaining nodes.

```
vagrant@db02:~$ sudo service mysql start
vagrant@db03:~$ sudo service mysql start
```

From any node you can query the cluster size to see that all three nodes are now members.

```
vagrant@db02:~$ sudo mysql -e "show status like
'wsrep_cluster_size';"
+--------------------+-------+
| Variable_name      | Value |
+--------------------+-------+
| wsrep_cluster_size | 3     |
+--------------------+-------+
```

Configuring the Cluster Check Utility

A **clustercheck** utility is included with Percona XtraDB Cluster. This allows the status of the cluster to be checked using an HTTP request on port 9200. If you look back at the HAProxy configuration you will see the following.

```
backend dbservers
     balance leastconn
     option httpchk
     server db01 192.168.12.61:3306 check port
9200 inter 12000 rise 3 fall 3
     server db02 192.168.12.62:3306 check port
9200 inter 12000 rise 3 fall 3 backup
     server db03 192.168.12.63:3306 check port
9200 inter 12000 rise 3 fall 3 backup
```

In order to allow requests to be processed by the utility we need to add an entry into the **/etc/services** file for it and enable **xinetd**. Perform these actions on all nodes in the database cluster.

```
vagrant@db01:~$ echo 'mysqlchk 9200/tcp #
mysqlchk' | sudo tee -a /etc/services
vagrant@db01:~$ sudo apt-get install -y xinetd

vagrant@db02:~$ echo 'mysqlchk 9200/tcp #
mysqlchk' | sudo tee -a /etc/services
vagrant@db02:~$ sudo apt-get install -y xinetd

vagrant@db03:~$ echo 'mysqlchk 9200/tcp #
mysqlchk' | sudo tee -a /etc/services
vagrant@db03:~$ sudo apt-get install -y xinetd
```

Finally, let's configure a database user so the utility can connect to the cluster and verify its operational status. Since this is a cluster you only have to create the user on one of the database nodes. Note that the password is "**clustercheckpassword!**" but you may need to escape the exclamation mark (\ !) as in the following example.

```
vagrant@db01:~$ sudo mysql -e "GRANT PROCESS ON
*.* TO 'clustercheckuser'@'localhost' IDENTIFIED
BY 'clustercheckpassword\!';"
vagrant@db01:~$ sudo mysql -e 'FLUSH PRIVILEGES;'
```

Now the **clustercheck** utility will respond when an HTTP request is sent to port 9200.

```
vagrant@db01:~$ curl localhost:9200
```

```
Percona XtraDB Cluster Node is synced.
vagrant@db01:~$ curl 192.168.12.62:9200
Percona XtraDB Cluster Node is synced.
vagrant@db01:~$ curl 192.168.12.63:9200
Percona XtraDB Cluster Node is synced.
vagrant@server01:~$ curl db01-private:9200
Percona XtraDB Cluster Node is synced.
```

In the event one of the nodes is not synced, the **clustercheck** utility will return "not synced."

```
vagrant@server01:~$ curl db02-private:9200
Percona XtraDB Cluster Node is not synced.
```

If you look at the HAProxy stats page you should see the database nodes are indeed ready to accept traffic.

Installing and Configuring WordPress

Now that the database cluster is configured we can create a user that will be used by our web application. Run the following commands on one of the database nodes.

```
vagrant@db01:~$ sudo mysql -e 'CREATE DATABASE
wordpress;'
vagrant@db01:~$ sudo mysql -e 'CREATE USER
wordpress IDENTIFIED BY "wordpress";'
vagrant@db01:~$ sudo mysql -e 'GRANT ALL
PRIVILEGES ON wordpress.* TO "wordpress";'
```

Next, choose one of the web servers to install the application files for WordPress. Remember that the storage is shared and synced across our nodes.

```
vagrant@server01:~$ cd /var/tmp
vagrant@server01:~$ wget -q
https://wordpress.org/latest.tar.gz
vagrant@server01:~$ tar xf /var/tmp/latest.tar.gz
-C /var/www
vagrant@server01:~$ chown -R www-data:www-data
/var/www/wordpress
vagrant@server01:~$ cd /var/www/wordpress
```

Specify the database connection information in
/var/www/wordpress/wp-config.php. Remember that the
local HAProxy process is configured to accept MySQL traffic and
proxy it to an available database node. This means you should set
the DB_HOST to 127.0.0.1.

```
vagrant@server01:~$ cp -p wp-config-sample.php
wp-config.php
vagrant@server01:~$ vi wp-config.php # And set
the following:
define('DB_NAME', 'wordpress');
define('DB_USER', 'wordpress');
define('DB_PASSWORD', 'wordpress');
define('DB_HOST', '127.0.0.1');
```

To complete the WordPress installation, open a web browser to the
VIP address (http://10.11.12.50). Follow the normal installation
process by answering a few questions. If you connect to any of the
database instances you will now see that WordPress database has
been populated and our database cluster is functioning.

```
vagrant@db01:~$ mysql -e 'show tables;' -u
wordpress -pwordpress wordpress
+----------------------+
| Tables_in_wordpress  |
```

```
+-----------------------+
| wp_commentmeta        |
| wp_comments           |
| wp_links              |
| wp_options            |
| wp_postmeta           |
| wp_posts              |
| wp_term_relationships |
| wp_term_taxonomy      |
| wp_terms              |
| wp_usermeta           |
| wp_users              |
+-----------------------+
```

Now let's make sure our file system is working as expected. Log into WordPress using the username and password you created. Go to the Media Library and upload a picture. I'm going to upload **cat-picture.jpg**. If you look on each of your web server nodes you'll find that picture on the filesystem.

```
vagrant@server01:~$ find /var/www/wordpress -name
cat-picture.jpg
/var/www/wordpress/wp-
content/uploads/2014/12/cat-picture.jpg
vagrant@server02:~$ find /var/www/wordpress -name
cat-picture.jpg
/var/www/wordpress/wp-
content/uploads/2014/12/cat-picture.jpg
```

Considerations for the Cloud

If you are going to be deploying this architecture in the cloud you will need to offload the work performed by Keepalived to your cloud provider. Instead of implementing a floating IP solution running on your servers you will need to use the cloud provider's load balancing service. For Amazon Web Services this is called an Elastic Load Balancer. Rackspace calls their service Cloud Load Balancers while Linode brands their solution NodeBalancers.

In any case, all of these cloud load balancers function very similarly. When you create a load balancer it will have a IP address associated with it. You will use that IP address as the DNS name for your web site. Configure the load balancer to accept HTTP traffic on port 80 and forward that traffic to port 8080 on each of your web server nodes. This configuration bypasses HAProxy and talks directly to your web servers. For this reason make sure you have health checks enabled on your cloud load balancer. You don't want to route traffic to a web server that is down. Also remember that you still need a HAProxy running on each of your web servers to connect to your backend database servers. Here's a diagram of what this solution looks like.

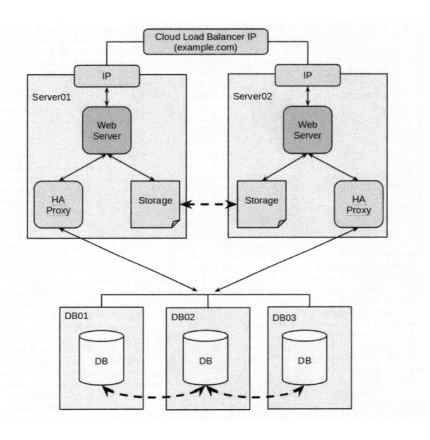

If you wanted, you could shift the web server to listen on the standard port of 80 and remove the HAProxy configuration for HTTP traffic. You could also eliminate HAProxy altogether and create another load balancer to serve database traffic. If you do, remember to update your application's configuration to point to the load balancer.

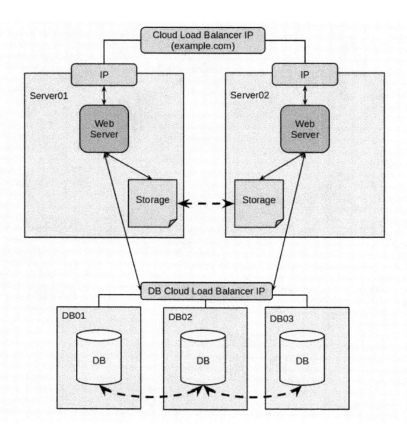

Scaling

Web Servers

To add another web server we will need to install apache, configure it as a Gluster client, and update the load balancer configuration.

Install apache, configure it to listen on port 8080, and add the configuration for your web site.

```
vagrant@server03:~$ sudo apt-get install -y
apache2 php5 php5-mysql
```

Here are the contents of **/etc/apache2/ports.conf**.

```
# If you just change the port or add more ports
here, you will likely also
# have to change the VirtualHost statement in
```

```
# /etc/apache2/sites-enabled/000-default.conf

#Listen 80
Listen 8080

<IfModule ssl_module>
     Listen 443
</IfModule>

<IfModule mod_gnutls.c>
     Listen 443
</IfModule>
```

Create **/etc/apache2/sites-available/wordpress.conf**
with the following contents.

```
LogFormat "%{X-Forwarded-For}i %l %u %t \"%r\"
%>s %b \"%{Referer}i\" \"%{User-Agent}i\""
haproxy_combined

<virtualhost *:8080>
  DocumentRoot /var/www/wordpress

  <Location />
     Options -Indexes
  </Location>

  ErrorLog ${APACHE_LOG_DIR}/wordpress_error.log
  LogLevel warn
  CustomLog
${APACHE_LOG_DIR}/wordpress_access.log
haproxy_combined
</virtualhost>
```

Enable this configuration and disable the default configuration. Also let's enable mod_rewrite for Wordpress.

```
vagrant@server03:~$ sudo a2ensite wordpress
vagrant@server03:~$ sudo a2dissite 000-default
vagrant@server03:~$ sudo a2enmod rewrite
vagrant@server03:~$ sudo service apache2 reload
```

Install the gluster client.

```
vagrant@server03:~$ sudo apt-get install -y
glusterfs-client
```

Add the entries of the storage servers to `/etc/hosts`.

```
vagrant@server03:~$ echo '192.168.12.51 server01-private' |
sudo tee -a /etc/hosts
vagrant@server03:~$ echo '192.168.12.52 server02-private' |
sudo tee -a /etc/hosts
```

Add an entry to `/etc/fstab` and mount the Gluster volume. Note that it doesn't really matter which storage server you specify for the mount point as the Gluster native client simply retrieves the volume file from that server. The volume file contains the other members of the storage cluster and Gluster will the best communication path.

```
vagrant@server03:~$ echo "server01-private:/var-
www /var/www glusterfs defaults,_netdev,fetch-
attempts=5 0 0" | sudo tee -a /etc/fstab
vagrant@server03:~$ sudo mv /var/www{,.orig}
vagrant@server03:~$ sudo mkdir /var/www
vagrant@server03:~$ sudo mount /var/www
```

Install and enable haproxy. We'll need it to proxy requests to the database cluster.

```
vagrant@server03:~$ sudo apt-get install -y
haproxy
vagrant@server03:~$ sudo sed -i.orig
's/ENABLED=.*/ENABLED=1/' /etc/default/haproxy
```

Take the existing haproxy configuration and append this server's
information to the web server section. Use that configuration on
the load balancers and this node. If you're using the cloud then
follow your cloud providers documentation. If you are using
HAProxy, here is what the **/etc/haproxy/haproxy.cfg** file will
look like.

```
global
      log 127.0.0.1 local0 notice
      user haproxy
      group haproxy


defaults
      log    global
      option    dontlognull
      retries 3
      option redispatch
      timeout connect   5000
      timeout client   50000
      timeout server   50000

frontend http
      bind *:80
      mode http
      option httplog
      default_backend webservers

backend webservers
      mode http
      stats enable
```

```
        stats uri /haproxy/stats
        stats auth admin:admin
        stats hide-version
        balance roundrobin
        option httpclose
        option forwardfor
        cookie SRVNAME insert
        server server01 192.168.12.51:8080 check
cookie server01
        server server02 192.168.12.52:8080 check
cookie server02
        server server03 192.168.12.53:8080 check
cookie server03

frontend sql
        bind *:3306
        mode tcp
        option tcplog
        default_backend dbservers

backend dbservers
        balance leastconn
        option httpchk
        server db01 192.168.12.61:3306 check port
9200 inter 12000 rise 3 fall 3
        server db02 192.168.12.62:3306 check port
9200 inter 12000 rise 3 fall 3 backup
        server db03 192.168.12.63:3306 check port
9200 inter 12000 rise 3 fall 3 backup
```

Reload the HAProxy configuration on each of the nodes. (Or restart HAProxy on the new node if you are using an external load balancer.)

```
vagrant@server01:~$ sudo service haproxy reload
vagrant@server02:~$ sudo service haproxy reload
```

```
vagrant@server03:~$ sudo service haproxy reload
```

Database Servers

Remember that you need an odd number of quorum votes for your
database cluster. This means the total number of database nodes
needs to be an odd number or you need to use the Galera arbitrator,
garbd. In many causes it might make more sense to scale the
databases vertically. Take one node down, increase its resources,
and bring it back up and let it rejoin the cluster. You could also take
one node down and replace it with another node that has more
resources.

To add another node to the database tier install Percona XtraDB
Cluster, create the my.cnf file, and start the database. It's that
simple. Also, remember to add this new node to your load balancer,
be that HAProxy or your cloud provider's solution.

```
vagrant@db04:~$ sudo apt-get install -y percona-
xtradb-cluster-server percona-xtradb-cluster-
galera-2.x
vagrant@db04:~$ sudo service mysql stop
```

The contents of **/etc/mysql/my.cnf** will be almost identical on
all of the nodes. The only difference will be the value of
wsrep_node_address. It should be set to the private IP of the
node. Add the private IP address of this node to the
wsrep_cluster_address line on all the database nodes. Here is
the **my.cnf** for db04.

```
[mysqld]
datadir=/var/lib/mysql
user=mysql
```

```
# Path to the Galera library.
wsrep_provider=/usr/lib/libgalera_smm.so

# Cluster connection URL contains the private IPs
all nodes.
wsrep_cluster_address=gcomm://192.168.12.61,192.1
68.12.62,192.168.12.63,192.168.12.64

# In order for Galera to work correctly binlog
format should be ROW.
binlog_format=ROW

# MyISAM storage engine has only experimental
support
default_storage_engine=InnoDB

# This changes how InnoDB autoincrement locks are
managed and is a requirement for Galera
innodb_autoinc_lock_mode=2

# SST method
wsrep_sst_method=xtrabackup

# Cluster name
wsrep_cluster_name=my_lamp_cluster

# Authentication for SST method
wsrep_sst_auth="sstuser:sstuser"

# db04 private IP address
wsrep_node_address=192.168.12.64
```

Start the database process on the new node.

```
vagrant@db04:/etc/mysql$ sudo service mysql start
```

Make sure the node has joined the cluster. The cluster size should increment by one.

```
vagrant@db04:/etc/mysql$ sudo mysql -e "show
status like 'wsrep_cluster_size';"
```

Setup the clustercheck utility by adding a line to /etc/services and installing xinetd.

```
vagrant@db04:~$ echo 'mysqlchk 9200/tcp #
mysqlchk' | sudo tee -a /etc/services
vagrant@db04:~$ sudo apt-get install -y xinetd
```

On each of the web server nodes add this new database to the database backends. Here is the HAProxy configuration for the database section that goes in **/etc/haproxy/haproxy.cfg**.

```
frontend sql
      bind *:3306
      mode tcp
      option tcplog
      default_backend dbservers

backend dbservers
      balance leastconn
      option httpchk
      server db01 192.168.12.61:3306 check port
9200 inter 12000 rise 3 fall 3
      server db02 192.168.12.62:3306 check port
9200 inter 12000 rise 3 fall 3 backup
      server db03 192.168.12.63:3306 check port
9200 inter 12000 rise 3 fall 3 backup
```

```
    server db04 192.168.12.64:3306 check port
9200 inter 12000 rise 3 fall 3 backup
```

Remember to reload the HAProxy configuration after it has been changed.

```
vagrant@server01:~$ sudo service haproxy reload
vagrant@server02:~$ sudo service haproxy reload
vagrant@serverNN:~$ sudo service haproxy reload
```

Storage

One way you will need to scale your Gluster cluster is to increase the amount of free space in your existing **var-www** volume. To do these create two new bricks and add it to the volume. Since the data in the volume is replicated (replica = 2), you'll need to add storage two bricks at a time. First present a new disk to be used as a brick to each of the storage nodes. Next, create a file system on those disks with the following commands

```
vagrant@server01:~$ sudo mkfs.xfs -i size=512 -f
/dev/sdc
vagrant@server02:~$ sudo mkfs.xfs -i size=512 -f
/dev/sdc
```

Let's create a mount point for our Gluster disk, add an entry for it in /etc/fstab, and mount it.

```
vagrant@server01:~$ echo "/dev/sdc
/data/glusterfs/var-www/brick02 xfs defaults 0 0"
| sudo tee -a /etc/fstab
vagrant@server01:~$ sudo mkdir -p
/data/glusterfs/var-www/brick02
vagrant@server01:~$ sudo mount
/data/glusterfs/var-www/brick02
```

```
vagrant@server02:~$ echo "/dev/sdc
/data/glusterfs/var-www/brick02 xfs defaults 0 0"
| sudo tee -a /etc/fstab
vagrant@server02:~$ sudo mkdir -p
/data/glusterfs/var-www/brick02
vagrant@server02:~$ sudo mount
/data/glusterfs/var-www/brick02
```

Finally, add the bricks to our existing volume. You only need to run this command on one of the storage nodes. After you add the bricks you will see the size of the volume increase. No downtime is needed to perform this operation. If you need more space, simply add more bricks.

```
vagrant@server01:~$ sudo gluster volume add-brick
var-www server01-private:/data/glusterfs/var-
www/brick02/brick  server02-
private:/data/glusterfs/var-www/brick02/brick
```

You don't have to add bricks on the same set of servers. You can put the storage on two new nodes that are dedicated to just serving storage or install the Gluster server software on another pair of web server nodes. First, add the new nodes IP information to **/etc/hosts** on each of the nodes in the storage cluster. The **/etc/hosts** file should contain:

```
192.168.12.51 server01-private
192.168.12.52 server02-private
192.168.12.53 server03-private
192.168.12.54 server04-private
```

Install the Gluster server software on the new storage nodes.

```
vagrant@server03:~$ sudo apt-get install -y
xfsprogs
vagrant@server03:~$ sudo apt-get install -y
glusterfs-server

vagrant@server04:~$ sudo apt-get install -y
xfsprogs
vagrant@server04:~$ sudo apt-get install -y
glusterfs-server
```

Use the **gluster peer probe** command from an existing member of the storage cluster to increase the size of your cluster.

```
vagrant@server01:~$ sudo gluster peer probe
server03-private
vagrant@server01:~$ sudo gluster peer probe
server04-private
vagrant@server01:~$ sudo gluster peer status
Number of Peers: 3

Hostname: server02-private
Uuid: 67bd33ae-4db4-476b-a135-b6e806d8bcb9
State: Peer in Cluster (Connected)

Hostname: server03-private
Uuid: c355c874-194a-48d1-be33-c0e83d127d7d
State: Peer in Cluster (Connected)

Hostname: server04-private
Uuid: 0e0bf8df-a107-4df8-8a1e-af274e21cfe8
State: Peer in Cluster (Connected)
```

Now you add bricks as before, but on the new storage nodes. Here's a quick recap of how to do that.

```
vagrant@server03:~$ sudo mkfs.xfs -i size=512 -f
/dev/sdb
vagrant@server04:~$ sudo mkfs.xfs -i size=512 -f
/dev/sdb

vagrant@server03:~$ echo "/dev/sdb
/data/glusterfs/var-www/brick03 xfs defaults 0 0"
| sudo tee -a /etc/fstab
vagrant@server03:~$ sudo mkdir -p
/data/glusterfs/var-www/brick03
vagrant@server03:~$ sudo mount
/data/glusterfs/var-www/brick03

vagrant@server04:~$ echo "/dev/sdb
/data/glusterfs/var-www/brick04 xfs defaults 0 0"
| sudo tee -a /etc/fstab
vagrant@server04:~$ sudo mkdir -p
/data/glusterfs/var-www/brick04
vagrant@server04:~$ sudo mount
/data/glusterfs/var-www/brick04

vagrant@server03:~$ sudo gluster volume add-brick
var-www server03-private:/data/glusterfs/var-
www/brick03/brick  server04-
private:/data/glusterfs/var-www/brick04/brick
```

If you see an error message like "Transport endpoint is not
connected" it was more than likely caused by a network
interruption. These types of errors are more likely when you are
testing with many virtual machines running on your local
workstation than it is to occur on production networks. In any case,
to recover from this error simply unmount and remount the file
system. Here's an example:

```
vagrant@server01:~$ cd /var/www
-bash: cd: /var/www: Transport endpoint is not
connected
vagrant@server01:~$ sudo umount /var/www
vagrant@server01:~$ sudo mount /var/www
```

Conclusion

I hope this book has not only helped you with the LAMP stack but it has shown you how you can tackle similar problems in the future. No matter what project you're working on it helps to be mindful of availability, redundancy, scalability, performance, and manageability.

If you would like to take the video training course based on the material in this book, visit:
http://www.linuxtrainingacademy.com/ha-lamp-stack.

All the best,

Jason

About the Author

Jason Cannon started his career as a Unix and Linux System Engineer in 1999. Since that time he has utilized his Linux skills at companies such as Xerox, UPS, Hewlett-Packard, and Amazon.com. Additionally, he has acted as a technical consultant and independent contractor for small businesses as well as Fortune 500 companies.

Jason has professional experience with CentOS, RedHat Enterprise Linux, SUSE Linux Enterprise Server, and Ubuntu. He has used several Linux distributions on personal projects including Debian, Slackware, CrunchBang, and others. In addition to Linux, Jason has experience supporting proprietary Unix operating systems including AIX, HP-UX, and Solaris.

He enjoys teaching others how to use and exploit the power of open source software. Jason is the author of *Command Line Kung Fu*, *Python Programming for Beginners*, and *Linux for Beginners* . He is also

the founder of the Linux Training Academy
(http://www.LinuxTrainingAcademy.com) where he blogs and
teaches online video training courses.

Other Books by the Author

Command Line Kung Fu
http://www.linuxtrainingacademy.com/command-line-kung-fu-book

Python Programming for Beginners
http://www.linuxtrainingacademy.com/python-book

Linux for Beginners
http://www.linuxtrainingacademy.com/linux

Courses by the Author

High Availability for the LAMP Stack
http://www.linuxtrainingacademy.com/ha-lamp-stack/

Linux for Beginners
http://www.linuxtrainingacademy.com/lfb-udemy

Learn Linux in 5 Days
http://www.linuxtrainingacademy.com/linux-in-5-days

Appendix

Popular Open Source Applications Based on the LAMP Stack

Bugzilla
Drupal
Etherpad Lite
Gitlab
Joomla
MediaWiki
Moodle
OwnCloud
phpBB
PunBB
Redmine
SugarCRM
Trac
Twiki
WordPress
Zen Cart

www.ingramcontent.com/pod-product-compliance
Lightning Source LLC
Chambersburg PA
CBHW071030050326
40689CB00014B/3590